CHAPTERS

IT'S TIME TO MOVE ON TO WHAT'S NEXT IN LIFE

MICHAEL JAMES RICE

Chapters: It's Time To Move On To What's Next In Life

Copyright © 2020 by Michael James Rice

First printing September 2020

All Scripture quotations, unless otherwise indicated, are taken from the New King James Version. Copyright © by Thomas Nelson Inc.

Published by Michael J Rice

9267 State Route 43

Streetsboro, Ohio 44241

ISBN 978-0-578-53227-1

Cover picture Shutterstock. Used with permission

Cover design by Sam Art Studio

Printed in the United States of America

All inquiries about reprinting and or translating into other languages should be addressed to Michael James Rice

Finding someone to dedicate this book to was easy.
My life has been filled with countless people who have all played roles
big and small in shaping who I am. Family, friends, fellow believers, and
even strangers. To every one of them I owe a debt of gratitude.
Nobody has played as instrumental role in my life as my treasure, my
wife Gale Beth. When we met, I was wandering like a drum looking for a
beat and my heart found it's rhythm in her. While I was still searching,
she was patient and willing to answer my endless questions with Godly
wisdom. We have shared our journey together for more than 35 years.
Our life has been filled with more than our share of laughs, more tears
than we would have chosen for ourselves, and enough adventures to keep
life from being boring.
To my son Gabriel who made this young man a father and whose care
compelled me to become a better man. I love you more than you know.
To Josiah, the son of my old age, who made me a young man again. I
love you too.
To my daughter in law Alisha your quiet, deep walk with God is
inspiring.
To my daughter in law Erin, what a joy it has been to watch you blossom
into the woman of God you are.
And to all those down through the years that have allowed me to grow in
my life as a pastor.

CONTENTS

FOREWORD

From the author:

For as long as I remember I have had a hearing problem. When someone said to me "you can't do that" or "it's never been done before", I heard, "this is what you should do". A book is to have one foreword, they say. I have three men who I have great respect for and who have made an impact in my life. It just seemed fitting to have each of them weigh in on my life's work. So, there are three forwards:

Many people get stuck in life, unfortunately some stay that way. They take on a victim mindset and waste precious time, sometimes years blaming others. Mike uses different parables Jesus used in teaching others how to get rid of wrong thinking and take on a new mentality that launches you into the direction that God planned for you from the beginning of time.

I admire and respect the wisdom that God has placed on Mike. The way he articulates the truths God has given to him to release to others is refreshing and captivating at the same time. I was encouraged and challenged as I read this book and I know you will be also. As you read be prepared for God to give you fresh insight and revelation of His unconditional love and acceptance He has for you.

Perhaps you are one that finds yourself trapped or stuck in life and has believed the lie that there's no way out. As you read on you'll find there is a way. Enjoy your new journey to freedom. Real freedom.

Jim White

Founder of White Unto Harvest Ministries

While completing my doctorate last year, I was researching for material from someone who could explain Nehemiah's leadership behavior. Among the available vast library, I found the writings of a Methodist pastor who was so helpful to my work. After mining out the parts I needed, I began to cite the work and discovered the entry was penned in 1897! It moved me to imagine a dedicated pastor in his study late one night, penning the words I was reading and hoping that the message would reach it's intended audience. There is no way he could have known that his words and efforts would last more than 120 years and another pastor in Northeast Ohio would need something he was inspired to write.

God does that.

It may be that God has done that for you through my friend Michael Rice. Human beings who loved God and were keenly dedicated to the Kingdom of God were moved by the Holy Spirit to pen the words we now refer to in our Bible. The Apostle Paul points out to Pastor Timothy that the Scriptures were inspired by the Holy Spirit (2 Timothy 3:16) and the Apostle Peter adds that God's prophets spoke as they were moved by the Holy Spirit to speak (2 Peter 1:21) and so it is that I affirm God is speaking through Michael Rice to an audience bigger than he or any of us can imagine.

I recommend your reading of this book.

It is an excellent treatment of the topic with some great provocative lines. Here are a few of my favorites…

God doesn't seem to understand our need for straight lines.

— Chapter 2

Straight lines—how we wish for more straight-line moments! Our life often feels like spaghetti and the tangled paths make us dizzy in the pursuit of life. Michael gets it and help us to see how our chase for organized, neat, chaos-free living gets in the way of what God is shaping in us—a life of deep and abiding trust born in the heat of confusing times. This trust is in a God who never panics, never stresses and wants us to be free to live life as He knows we should...we just have to surrender to it.

...a bruise is not a sign of healing but is indication of a wound.

— CHAPTER 3

On my right hand is a scar that reminds me of the day more than 50 years ago when I picked up a soft drink bottle and played with it as a sword to my younger counterpart. The resulting injury took a long time to heal because of its location near the base of my index finger and even now the ugly scar reminds me of the past experience, but it doesn't hurt anymore!

We all have scars and reminders of where we have been, what we have suffered, and how we have overcome. If we have trusted Jesus to heal us, take the initiative to forgive those who hurt us and refused to be defined by yesterday, we can be proud of our scars. They are trophies of God's grace at work in us, helping us to be everything God has wanted us to be.

Michael unpacks the power of forgiveness in a way that can help you and me. Take time to read and embrace the words intellectually but listen with your heart to the whisper of the Spirit urging you to move ahead and grasp the next chapter.

God's goal is to get you into heaven, but He is not in a hurry to do it.

— Chapter 6

I've often wondered why God doesn't just take us to heaven the moment we are saved. That makes sense to me and avoids a lifetime of heartache, pain and sorrow. However, Michael is right—God is using your life as a witness and the Apostle Paul says as much to Pastor Timothy (1 Timothy 1:12-16). Your life and mine is a living, visible demonstration of God's grace and what happens when someone is completely surrendered to God's will. So the day to day events, the struggles and moments that take our breath away serve to bring about a greater glory to the cause of Christ and help the unbeliever to know what God can do in them!

I'm an avid reader and for much of my life I have had a personal goal of two books a month, though there are times when I don't make my goal. The format of books allows for each chapter to build toward the next and there is anticipation as you read deeper into the story. The author compels you to keep going, to read further and explore more and more. Michael does that also and each chapter builds your understanding and hope. Because I was given the privilege of an early review, I know where you are going, I know what you are going to read—but I don't have the foreknowledge to know what it is going to do for you. So, here's a couple of personal suggestions and my prayer…

Read the book to understand yourself and personalize everything you read at the point to ask "is this something God is doing in me?" and work on daily application.

Keep notes. As I get older, I'm realizing how important journaling is with my relationship to God and how important notetaking is to study and reading. If you don't write it down as God nudges you, you will not remember it—so take notes!

My prayer is that you will find transformation. When I write, I ask

God to do what I cannot do—put the book into the hands of the people for whom the message was intended. I know the author and I'm pretty confident that is his prayer as well. His writing is not about notoriety but obedience and his fulfillment and joy will be in hearing that God has done powerful things in you and others as they read.

I commend my friend and fellow pastor, Michael Rice. I've known him since 2008 and his dedication to the Gospel and to his community is noted and appreciated. He's a faithful husband, a great father, an outstanding pastor and leader and now an accomplished author.

What's your next chapter?

William E. (Bill) Isaacs
Madison, Ohio
2020

————

Every once in a while, I come across a book that grabs my attention on page one and doesn't let go until I finish the book. Michael Rice's book "Chapters, It's Time To Move On To What's Next In Life", is that type of book. The reading is easy; the thought process is challenging as you move through nine chapters of an author sharing his heart, and more importantly sharing the heart of Father God. The book is full of interesting takes on familiar scriptures that caused me to stop and think and rejoice about the relationship I have with my Heavenly Father.

I have known the author for at least 30 years and I'm not surprised by the authenticity of his message. Michael is a great pastor and speaker. Michael is also a good friend. The kind of friend everyone needs. The kind of friend who is genuinely honest and full of compassion. A friend who is not afraid to tell you the truth because he believes the truth will, if received, set you free.

I'm confident the investment of your time in reading this book is worthwhile. For some it will be a beautiful reminder of God and His plans for your life. For others the book's messages will be life-changing, if received with the same thought-provoking intensity with which it was written. I encourage you to pour yourself a cup of coffee and prepare your heart, in a quiet place, to hear from your Father as you enjoy this message of hope regardless of what season of life you find yourself in.

Donald Knipp
Pastor Emeritus, Christian Life Church Mentor Ohi

INTRODUCTION

Have you ever felt stuck?

Like there must be something more, better, than what I am experiencing right now? You know there is something better for you, but it just seems like there are things happening or that have happened to you that are preventing you from getting "there".

Our creator designed our life to move towards a desired fulfilling, challenging, and adventurous life. A steady march of improvement towards who he has created us to be, and the life we were destined to live.

The chapters of our life have been ordained to occur in an orderly fashion, but they rarely do. We often get stuck between or within chapters and our lives become stale or worse.

We have all enjoyed a stream of water as it trickles by. The sound the water makes can be so relaxing and soothing. That sound is made because there is movement, progress if you will.

A closer look reveals that there are places where the flow of the stream is interrupted by a turn of direction or something intruding into the stream. Behind each of those is usually a gathering of debris. At one point the debris was making progress and was part of the life of the stream. But now it is stuck and unless something happens to break it free, it will slowly just be worn down by the ongoing rush of water.

Some of you reading this can relate. Your life took an unexpected turn. Something happened or someone came along, and you have never been the same. You have never felt " right" since. Life happens around you, you may even enjoy the noise of it but in the quiet moments you feel very stuck and very alone.

God did not design us to be stuck or alone but alone and stuck we often are. Loneliness is easy to identify but how do we know when we are stuck? When the comfort of our present misery is greater than the passion of our hope to move forward, we are stuck.

Being stuck is miserable. Miserable for us and miserable for those who have to deal with us. Being stuck is dangerous and can literally make us sick. Sick of our job, family, marriage, sick of life. People often do stupid things when they are stuck, which usually just makes them more stuck. Like flailing in the midst of quicksand we are placated by the struggle but seem oblivious to the reality we are only getting more stuck.

Can this book help you?

Not in the usual sense of a self-help book where the author tells the reader what to do and success is dependent upon the reader properly carrying out those directives. If the step by step self-help books worked, then why are so many new ones being written every year?

Besides if we could self-help would we still be stuck?

Unlike most books where one needs to read the chapters in order, I would suggest that you read them in whatever order works for you. The Holy Spirit is the agent of the Godhead that is tasked with guiding us into truth. Ask Him for direction while looking at the Table of Contents. Read first the chapter that seems to capture your attention. He knows you better than you know yourself and He loves to help.

This book was written in the solitude of nature, in my truck, in my bedroom, or the quiet noise of a nearby coffee shop. This book is about life, and it was written while life was ever present. Much of it written while fasting so I may clearly hear from God.

Hemingway has been quoted as saying there is nothing to writing, just sit down at your typewriter and bleed. That seems dramatic but I kind of understand. This book has been in the works for years, in fact most of my life. I am not sure if I am writing this book or God is writing it through me. Something beyond me has unfailingly compelled me forward. My hesitation to write is found in the fact that many smart and gifted people have written books, I am neither. After all that has been written what could I possibly add? Seriously, I am nobody. Besides, I can be lazy, and writing is work.

And yet God would not let me avoid it.

As I have written these truths I have laughed, winced and even cried when I thought of the experiences I had so I could learn these truths, and prayed from my heart that you would know his heart for you in whatever you face. It is my sincere belief and hope that the truths shared in this book will trigger releases that resonate through your spirit. Those truths which were placed inside of you when you were fearfully and wonderfully made simply need to be awakened. God has let me know he fully intends to use this book to trigger things inside the readers of it.

The power to be free is already in us.

Doesn't it just make sense that God would design us that way? You have been designed and created for, ordained to good works. Each chapter of this book is inspired to cause you to have a "whoa" moment. You will know these truths and as you read them here, they will settle into you like a longtime friend. Truth on its own will not make us free any more than sleeping with a bible under our pillow will give us bible knowledge. Only when truth becomes personal to us, when we "know" it, is its power to deliver us released. You will know these truths and you will be free!

1

YOU KNOW ME

He was known as Roy "Wrong Way" Riegels. Riegels played on the 1928 University of California (Cal) Golden Bears football team. Cal's coach Nibs Price gave credit to Riegels as the smartest player he ever coached.

On January 1, 1929, the Golden Bears faced the Georgia Tech Yellow Jackets at the Rose Bowl in Pasadena, California, USA. Midway through the second quarter, Riegels picked up a fumble by Tech's Jack "Stumpy" Thomason. Just 30 yards away from the Yellow Jackets' end zone, Riegels was somehow turned around and ran 69 yards in the wrong direction. The following describes what transpired from Riegels perspective: "I was running toward the sidelines when I picked up the ball," Riegels told The Associated Press. "I started to turn to my left toward Tech's goal. Somebody shoved me and I bounded right off into a tackler. In pivoting to get away from him, I completely lost my bearings."

Teammate Benny Lom chased Riegels, screaming at him to stop. Known for his speed, Lom finally caught up with Riegels at California's 3-yard line and tried to turn him around, but he was immediately hit by a wave of Tech players and tackled back to the 1-yard line. The Golden Bears chose to punt rather than risk a play so close to their own end zone, but Georgia Tech blocked the punt for a safety, giving them a 2–0 lead.

During Roy's wrong way run, Georgia Tech's coach Bill Alexander said to his excited players who were jumping up and down near the Tech bench: "Sit down. Sit Down. He is just running the wrong way. Every step he takes is to our advantage". Broadcaster Graham McNamee, who was calling the game said during Roy's wrong way run: "What am I seeing? What is wrong with me? Am I crazy? Am I crazy? Am I crazy?" Georgia Tech would ultimately win the game—and their second national championship—8–7.

Roy's problem was not caused by stupidity, lack of desire or effort. In his own words he said someone shoved him early in his run and got him all turned around. After that, his desire, effort and skill actually worked against him. I think that is how it is with some of us, maybe you.

We are not stuck because we haven't tried to move forward, we are stuck because we got shoved in the wrong direction and our efforts and passions have made matters worse.

Follow me on this.

Most believers would sum up our start in life something like this: Life began when a sperm fertilized an egg and I started to grow. I was born with a sinful nature, destined to be eternally separated from God. Unless God intervened, I would stumble through life hopeless until at some point I was presented with and accepted an opportunity to begin believing in a God I had never met and of whom I know almost nothing.

Without that opportunity and my correct response, I was hopeless of ever coming to know God and would be eternally tormented for my sinful nature, which by the way, I never chose.

Punished by a God I had never met, never fully understanding why.

For the record I believe that we have all been born in sin, and without redemption we will be eternally separated from God. I get it.

Yet if our understanding is that this is how we got our start and how it works does that not strike you as like the worst plan ever? It's almost like a game of spiritual Russian Roulette with eternal consequences. What if I never hear about God's plan? What if I don't grasp the gravity of my decision? I have a million more what ifs. To hear some tell the story we are just flung out there into life not only covered in sin, it flows through us like a flood and we have no real compass to find our way. The odds are stacked against us having any hope of finding God. Very few ever do.

Occasionally there are divine interruptions but, we spend most of our life just stumbling and bumbling. Bouncing off this experience bouncing off that relationship bouncing off that failed attempt to find the truth. And after years we find ourselves much like Pontius Pilate, "what is truth?" Boy talk about being shoved the wrong way!

Does that sound like the plan of a loving almighty God?

What would happen if we came to know that our beginning was much more hopeful and intentional? What if from the very beginning there was someone involved, who loves us, I mean really loves us? What if this God was thoughtful and loving and careful and designed our life to maximize the possibility of us finding our way to him or more accurately our way back to him? Wouldn't it help to know that somebody was for us and not against us, cheering for us, and doing everything possible to help us to find a way into heaven instead of seeming to find a way to keep us out?

What if we knew that from the very beginning His desire was that we win and not lose, that we succeed and not fail?

We know from the often quoted Jeremiah 29:11 that God has thoughts toward us that are nothing but good. Thoughts about our future, our peace, and to give us hope (a reason to believe that things will get better).

One thing that had not been made clear to me was, when did those thoughts begin?

If we buy into the notion that they started at our birth then our thinking lines up with the abortionist, life begins at birth. Not ready to join that group I searched for a deeper meaning.

Or do we agree with the psalmist David who was a man who pursued neither the things of God nor the hand of God but the heart of God? David likely understood the thoughts of God better than most. God Himself called David a man after my own heart.

Lest you think David could not relate to your struggle or that he had a "normal" start to life, be reminded that David was the least of Jesse's sons and is thought by many to be the result of an affair that his father

Jesse had. Another misconception killer, he probably looked less like Richard Gere and more like Ron Howard (1 Samuel 17:42).

Writing under the inspiration of the Holy Spirit in Psalms 139:13 he paints a picture of a God intimately involved in our creation forming and covering. David uses a word that implies weaving. In Psalms 139:16 he says

"Your eyes saw my substance, being yet unformed. And in Your book they all were written, the days fashioned for me, when as yet there were none of them."

Let me say it this way:

The headlines of the newspaper of your life are in books already written on God's shelf. God is not solving the problem you face, he has already solved it.

Nothing has ever happened to you that your creator did not know about before you were born and rather than stop the painful experiences, he destined that everything would work together for your good. Always. The greater the pain, the greater the good.

David is saying that when we were yet unformed in our mother's womb God saw us there.

Before we had lived our first day on earth God knew all about our last day on earth, and every day in between. Wherever you are in your journey, whatever you face right now, allow this truth to settle into your spirit for just a moment.

It gets even better.

God speaking to Jeremiah took it a step further by saying in Jeremiah 1:5 "Before I formed you in the womb, I knew you;". *Before* God formed us in the womb God *knew* us.

That word knew is an interesting and powerful word. We see it early in scripture in Genesis 4:1 "Now Adam *knew* Eve his wife and she conceived . . .". It is a word used to describe an intimate relationship. It can also mean to be made known or become known, to be revealed.

When a husband knows a wife in that sense the result is that seeds from him are placed inside his wife. Those seeds carry with them the blueprint of his genetic makeup, his life. And that life is placed inside the woman to be woven together with her egg. And a new life is created. The life that is created has the DNA of the man and the DNA of the woman and takes on attributes of both.

It is unclear exactly what decides which attributes are dominant and which are recessive. This is a good example of what should be taking place in the believer's life. Through our intimacy with God, by means of prayer, reading His Word, fellowship with his Spirit, meditation and connectedness with his body the church, his life is placed inside of us. The result of that intimacy is that the seed of his Word not only grows inside of us and changes us, but it comes out of our bellies as rivers of living water to affect others and our world. This is more than a casual acquaintance; it is involved interaction.

God said he had that kind of relationship with us *before we were formed in our mother's womb. Read* that again.

God knew you intimately before you were born. And because it is impossible for someone to know you intimately without you knowing them intimately, God is no stranger to you.

What does all this mean? Let's look a little deeper.

When scripture says we have been reconciled to God the word reconciled means *returned* to a state of harmony, to restore to its original state. In other words, salvation is *restoring* us to a relationship we had with God before he formed us in our mother's womb. Frankly, I do not yet know what that all means, but the Holy Spirit took effort to ascertain we understood our beginnings were not an accident but rather quite intentional. When scripture says God knew me before I was in the womb, then he personally wove my inner most being together and saw all my days before even one had come to pass, that is an absolute truth. An absolute truth is absolutely true, whether or not we understand it.

That is a far cry from us being tossed out with little hope. We are not finding our way to God; we are finding our way *back* to Him. I believe there is a part of us that by instinct searches, seeks for God. We are born with a hunger, a thirst for him. Our spirit somehow still knows the way home. We may not know the route, but we know the Way. (You will catch that in a moment).

In one of the most moving chapters in scripture, John 14, Jesus is trying to quiet the storm caused in the hearts of His disciples by His revelation to them in John 13 when He said He would only be with them a little while longer. He tells them do not let your heart be troubled.

We humans get all kind of ways freaked out when someone talks about the unknown. But Jesus tells them that he will personally go and prepare a place for them. Then He says in John 14:4 "where I go you know and the way you know." There is that word again, they *know*.

Go ahead, look back and see. There is no record of Jesus telling them anything about going back to heaven or how they could follow him there. And yet he says this place I am going to, you *know*, and the way there, you *know*.

Thomas the doubter chimes in by saying we don't know where you are going, how can we know the way? Jesus comes out with those words we know so well "I am the way, the truth, and the life. No one comes to the Father except through Me. "If you had known Me, you would have known My Father also; and from now on you know Him and have seen Him." (John 14:6 -7 NKJV)

Could this be what Jesus is saying? Don't be afraid guys, I am not going off into the unknown, you know where I am going, and you know the way. We are going back home to Father and since you have known me, you have known him as well. In fact, from now on walk in this truth, you know Him and have seen Him. That is why I must go and the Spirit will be sent who will awaken your spirit, that part of you that knows God and is the primary part of you that "connects" with God.

When the Spirit of God comes to us it is much like when the disciples walked with Jesus on the road to Emmaus. In Luke 24 is the story of two men who were trying to make sense of all that had happened with the death and burial of Jesus. Suddenly He has joined them on their walk "But their eyes were restrained, so that they did not know Him." (Luke 24:16 NKJV).

He reproved them for not understanding why this all had to happen. They encourage him to spend the night with them and while having their evening meal he breaks bread and "Then their eyes were opened, and they knew Him; and He vanished from their sight." (Luke 24:31 NKJV).

Without the help of the Holy Spirit our eyes are restrained, and we don't know God. But when we spend time with him our eyes are opened, and we realize that we know him!

Here is a truth, you can't lose something you never had.

That being true then what other conclusion can we come to after reading the following?

For the Son of Man has come to save that which was lost.

— Matthew 18:11, NKJV

"What man of you, having a hundred sheep, if he loses one of them, does not leave the ninety-nine in the wilderness, and go after the one which is lost until he finds it? And when he has found it, he lays it on his shoulders, rejoicing. And when he comes home, he calls together his friends and neighbors, saying to them, 'Rejoice with me, for I have found my sheep which was lost!'

— Luke 15:4-6

As a young pastor I was asked to visit a lady in Riverside Methodist Hospital in Columbus, Ohio who was dying of cancer. She was not a believer and had no family.

Madeline was 88 years old and had lost her sight more than 40 years earlier to diabetes. I found her room and introduced myself. She was short and extremely emaciated because of the cancer. Maybe it was because she was lonely or maybe it was because of fear of her impending death, she talked non-stop.

After more than an hour I left after having said almost nothing. Knowing her time was short I visited again the next day and the next hoping to talk to her about God and His incredible love for her but each day I left defeated.

Every attempt to engage her was met with her just talking over me. I just did not have what it took to quiet her long enough to talk with her about God. Having been taught to respect your elders I felt I was doing the right thing by listening to her.

Burdened by the nearness of her death and not having any reason to believe that she had faith in God I asked God to help me get through to her as she didn't appear to have long to live. My next visit started like all the others and out of sheer desperation I rose from my chair made my way across the room to her bed and sat down on the side of her bed at her waist and interrupted her by saying

Madeline, I need you to be quiet, I need to talk with you about something. She seemed as startled as I was by my intrusion into her personal space. Hospital visitation 101 taught me NEVER SIT ON THE BED!

But sitting on the bed I was.

For the next 30 minutes I poured out my heart to her about God's love, her sin, repentance and forgiveness. She sat still and never offered a peep until I finished by asking her if she would like to pray.

With a passion that betrayed deeply held emotion, her voice was somewhere between a rebuke and a cry of deep pain she yelled at me "what took you so long?". I wasn't sure I understood, but before I could gather the courage to ask her what she meant she told me her story.

As an infant she was an only child and had lost both of her parents. Her grandparents stepped up to raise her and she described them as loving, kind, and faithful church attenders. Madeline had never married and now had no known living relatives. One night when Madeline was 8 years old, and a few short months before she too unexpectedly passed away, grandma was tucking Madeline in bed. Grandma seemed pensive as she sat on the side of the bed and told Madeline this.

"Madeline, today as I prayed for you God showed me something. I saw you lying in a bed and a young man sits down on the side of your bed and tells you to be quiet because he has something important to talk to you about. Listen closely to what he has to say and when he asks you if you want to pray, Maddie, tell him yes!"

Madeline then begins weeping and she again yells at me "I have been waiting for you 80 years, what took you so long?" I can't even begin to get my head around the reality that more than 50 years before I was born, years before my parents were born, God showed Maddie's grandma that He would send me to this child to tell her about Him.

Madeline joined the family of God that day.

The next day I visited Madeline again, not knowing it would be the last time I would see her this side of heaven.

As I walked into her room she was laying in her bed, still blind, still swollen with cancer, but her arms were both lifted in the air and she was crying tears of joy, "isn't God good to us?" she said as she laughed and cried and carried on. I can't explain, nor do I have words to describe it, but she was not acting like somebody who had known God less than 24 hours. The passion and intimacy she shared with him betrayed something far older and much deeper.

Maybe what the scripture is trying to tell us is we do not need to let our heart be troubled, things didn't start off as bad as we thought. Maybe our connection to God runs deeper than we have previously been led to believe. Finding our way back to God seems a far less daunting task than trying to discover someone we have never met and navigating a path we have never known. We know where we are going, and we know the Way.

Just as he chose us in him before the foundation of the world, that we should be holy and without blame before him in love, having predestined us to adoption as sons by Jesus Christ to himself, according to the good pleasure of his will, to the praise of the glory of his grace, by which he made us accepted in the beloved. (Ephesians 1:4-6 NKJV)

Wikipedia contributors. "Roy Riegels." Wikipedia, The Free Encyclopedia. Wikipedia, The Free Encyclopedia, 24 Jan. 2014. Web. 5 Mar. 2014

2

ROUND AND ROUND WE GO

As a child I had a strong dislike for merry-go-rounds. Believe me, now at my age the thought of getting on a metal disc and being spun until I am provided the opportunity to view the contents of my stomach is still not on my list of enjoyable things to do. Even before I had my fingers mangled and nearly tore off by one, I didn't like merry-go-rounds. Maybe it's because with a merry-go-round you never get anywhere. With the slide you start one place and you end up in another. With the monkey bars the same. Even with the swing if you're adventurous like me when you're done going back-and-forth you launch off at just right time and you land somewhere else feeling like Superman. Not so the merry-go-round. With it you go around and round and round and then you stop. You barely can hold on as this stupid thing tries to fling you off and when it finally stops you not only have not gotten anywhere, you are now sick! Some people call that fun!

And yet in a moment of honesty does that not seem like what happens in life all too often? We just go around and around having the same experiences making the same mistakes. The names, locations, and time changes but our experiences sometimes seem all too familiar. We have déjà vu of having déjà vu. It seems like some unseen force is just pulling on us and is trying to throw our life into a total mess, or worse, maybe it already has.

And when we have been on this merry-go-round for a while and not gotten anywhere, we just end up sick of it all. Frustrated is too kind a word. Sometimes hopeless, dejected, depressed are a better descriptors of how we feel.

When we were younger it just seemed like if we pushed harder, worked longer, tried something different, everything would work out. A new job, a new home, maybe a new spouse, we were willing to try anything. Take this vacation, buy this car, wear these clothes. Maybe it's their fault, maybe this place, maybe something is wrong with me. We find ourselves years maybe even decades later and we are still just going around and around and around. Why can't life be like, well, like taking a vacation? Our goal is to enjoy the experience, so we start out with a plan where we leave point A and arrive at point B. We pay what it costs, and we get an experience and then we move on. Nice neat orderly just the way we think life is supposed to be but often isn't.

We humans seem to like nice straight lines. A line means there is a plan, there is progress, there is production, there is an expected outcome. Look at almost everything we humans build. If we are not trying to bend to the laws of friction, think cars, boats, planes, we build things using lots of straight lines. Our houses, buildings, even this book you hold or the tablet your reading this on, straight lines everywhere. Point A to point B, nice and neat, orderly and efficient.

Yet, when it comes to matters of the heart, relationships, especially in our relationship with God and others, we struggle. We struggle because there are no straight lines. Our journey looks less like a ribbon of a highway and more like a bowl of spaghetti. We want to say something to another person and to be understood exactly as we meant it. We want to pray to God, have Him answer it the way that we asked without him changing things. We want life to be like a microwave, stick a problem in and press the buttons and in a little while it's finished.

And what makes it worse God doesn't seem to understand our need for straight lines. Nice neat orderly. Why can't he be more like us?

I mean, even the Bible says everything being done decently and in order. Why can't God orchestrate the affairs of my life and help with my relationships by applying some decently and in order?

Every time we try to fix things by establishing a deadline or giving somebody an ultimatum, it almost never seems to work.

Why doesn't God help me by changing those people or fixing these situations in my life right now the way I want them fixed?

Spoiler alert, God really does not like straight lines.

In fact, God's preferred method of operation in dealing with us is to keep us running around in circles . . . until. Here's the rub, we like straight lines, God likes circles. Until we learn about God and why He likes circles we will just keep running around in those circles.

Look at God's creation, nearly everything is circles with very few straight lines. From the proton, neutron and nucleus in the atom to a planet or the sun or even galaxies, everything is circles.

Not only are they circles they all seem to be going in circles. The neutron and proton circling the nucleus, the earth revolves around the sun, our galaxy is spinning through the universe. We humans are so stuck on everything being straight lines we used to think the earth was flat. Nope, it's a circle just like God wanted it to be.

The creation reflects the heart of the creator. By that we can tell that God really doesn't seem to like straight lines, because there are very few straight lines in nature. In the simplest terms an atom bomb is a result of us splitting an atom. We split the round atom by dissecting (there is our straight line), a nucleus with a neutron or proton. That pretty well sums up what happens in our life when we try to dissect God's circles with our straight lines. We blow everything up. You would think we would tire of having life blow up in our faces but until we come to the place that we accept the reality that God operates in circles we will always be frustrated in our relationship with him. For our sake we need to grab ahold of this truth. Both his goal and his perspective are very different than ours.

We want it fixed right now and we think a temporary fix is better than our temporary pain.

We are even willing at times to trade one pain for another instead of fixing the problem. I recently saw a bladder control medicine being advertised and the number one side effect is diarrhea. Nothing gets fixed, we just trade which end we leak from. To foolishly dive further into that analogy, the problem is not fixed we just change who sees we have a problem, those who we are approaching, or those we are walking away from. As funny as that is, it is metaphorically quite rich!

We are his workmanship which means God wants to fix us.

His approach sometimes seems contrary to logic because we are so absorbed in the right now and he always has his eyes on eternity because everything else passes away, but we live for an eternity.

God is so confident that he is right and so passionate about us that he will allow us to spin on the merry-go-round for decades . . . until.

The third chapter of the book of Ecclesiastes starts by describing the circles of time. I know we humans see time as linear, God describes it as seasons and to everything there is a season.

Then in the middle of the chapter he drops this bombshell of truth. "That which hath been is now; and that which is to be hath already been; and God requires that which is past" (Ecclesiastes 3:15 KJV). That is God's way of describing a circle. The thing from my past is now happening again, and the problem coming up is just like the problem I thought was behind me.

Why is this happening?

It's happening because God loves us, but we keep missing the whole point of our problem. God requires that we know the truth we keep passing over. Consequently, the problem will be back to visit us again and again until we know why it was there in the first place.

We think problems have come into our life and we need to fix them. God allows problems into our life to fix *us*.

God is not working on problems, he is working on us, we are His workmanship.

Problems are incredibly easy to solve for one who flung galaxies off his tongue.

But his greatest creation has proven a bigger challenge because he can't change us until he convinces us to change our will. We won't change our will until we know what is wrong with it. So, get ready because you will be back into this mess until you know why you were in it the first time.

A real subplot is played out with the disciples, Jesus, and boats. And frankly it gets kind of funny because it hits so close to home. The disciples never grasped the truth that Jesus wanted them to learn from boats. Think about it, nearly every time Jesus and the disciples interact with a boat it's a mess. The first is in Matthew 8 when Jesus gets into a boat and the disciples follow Him and a big storm pops up *immediately.* The disciples are frightened and seek the Lord's help and find him sleeping! They wake him in a panic by telling him they are about to perish. Before he speaks to their problem, he speaks to them. Something in them is the problem. God will require the truth they aren't grasping.

And you can bet they will circle back to a boat again because God requires they know the truth they passed over.

Jesus asks them why are you afraid? Then he answers his own question by telling them it's because they have little faith. He is telling them that the storm is not the problem, their lack of faith is. Then in Mark 6 He tells the disciples to get into a boat and he will meet them on the other side "Immediately He made His disciples get into the boat and go before Him to the other side, to Bethsaida, while He sent the multitude away.

— MARK 6:45, NKJV

The disciples begin to cross, and a storm pops up. Sound familiar? Only this time Jesus isn't in the boat, he's far away. There is a pattern I have noticed with God. When we revisit a problem because we didn't learn the first time, God is often more distant than he was previously. He is not uncaring; He is wanting to get our attention.

He is wanting us to depend on his Word when we can't feel His presence.

Much like a parent lets go of a child when the child is learning to walk.

As the disciples struggle with rowing for hours they look up and see

Jesus walking on the water and he isn't coming to help, in fact it looks like he is going to walk past them. He has no desire to fix their problem, he wants to fix what is wrong with them. He has not only told them previously what is wrong, he gave them the answer for this test when he told them what to do.

In every command from God there is a promise from God.

Did you catch the answer he gave then in that verse?

He told them to meet him on the other side. That means he had ordained they were going to make it to the other side. So, he is walking past them because he has established an appointment with them - on the other side- and there is no storm big enough to cancel that appointment. They were as sure to make it as he was, if they would just trust him.

Immediately before this story of the boat, the disciples had tried to solve the problem of a shortage of bread to feed five thousand by sending the people away. We often do that; we think someone else is the problem and if we could just send them away our problem is solved.

Jesus knew the people were not the problem any more than the storm was the problem.

The problem was in the heart of his disciples and the disciple Mark is starting to make the connection. He sees that the truth that evaded them concerning the bread is the same truth that is evading them about the boat. "Then He went up into the boat to them, and the wind ceased. And they were greatly amazed in themselves beyond measure, and marveled. ***For they had not understood about the loaves, because their heart was hardened.***"(Mark 6:51, 52 NKJV)

Our problems are rarely caused by the presence of something or someone but rather by the absence of something. The absence of a truth we need to know.

So, the disciples find themselves going from one boat in a storm to another boat in a storm. They go from one crowd of people that need bread to another crowd of people that need bread. These disciples get so shook up about boats and bread that one time while in a boat Jesus tells them to beware of the leaven of the Pharisees and they think Jesus is upset because they don't have any bread. Round and round they go, kind of like us sometimes. What is the answer to getting off the merry-go-round?

Actually, what *is* the answer.

All too often when things happen to us that we don't like, we ask God why? Why did this happen to me or even worse why did this happen to me again? God has already told us that we are his workmanship and that everything works together for our good if we are seeking His purpose in our life. Everything. When problems arise and we pull out a why and fling it at God it is not so much a question as it is an accusation. We want him to explain to us why this happened as if his motive could be anything but for our good.

Lose the why question with God. Start asking Him what.

What truth am I lacking that you are trying to teach me?

"If any of you lacks wisdom, let him ask of God, who gives to all liberally and without reproach, and it will be given to him."

— James 1:5, NKJV

God is so excited about moving you on to the next incredible chapter of your life that He is eager for you to ask Him so He can liberally give you the answer. He loves you and he is for you so ask him. Right now is a good time, ask Him. And you will become personally acquainted with the truth and that truth will set you free. Guaranteed.

3

TWO DAYS THAT WILL RUIN YOUR LIFE

This is the day The Lord has made we will rejoice and be glad in it.

There are two days that have the potential to absolutely ruin your life.

Everyone reading this book has one of them, most will have both.

Many of the struggles I have seen in our lives are because we just don't know how to handle these two days. It will be tempting to skip this chapter thinking this doesn't apply to you but that would be a mistake. At the end of the chapter I ask a very probing question you need to answer to yourself. Only then will you be sure these two days are not ruining your life.

The first day that will ruin your life is tomorrow.

While on a family drive in the country we came across a self-storage business that had a recreational vehicle out front for sale. What struck us was the enormity of it and its location on a small country road. Not having any expectation of buying it we stopped to look inside just to see what it was like. This thing was like a palace on wheels! It had Amish custom cabinets, slide outs, hydraulic levelers, security system, awnings, nothing was left out. Even though it was nearly 10 years old it was like brand new inside and out. When I looked at the odometer, I realized why it looked so good, it had just over 3,000 miles on it. On the counter in the kitchen was the original price sticker showing a cost of over a quarter of a million dollars.

We hoped to get on our way before anybody came out and discovered us looking at a camper that was far beyond our ability to buy, but we were too slow. Not wanting the salesman to ask why people driving a five-hundred-dollar car are looking at a vehicle of this price I distracted him by asking him to tell me about the RV. The story he told was tragic. The RV was owned by a friend of his, a widow.

For many years, her husband worked as an executive in a major firm in Cincinnati, Ohio.

Worked is not the right word. He was addicted to his job. He repeatedly placated the dissatisfaction of his wife when she complained of them never having time together. "When I retire, I will buy us the nicest motor home you can find and we will tour the country, just you and me". The hope of that was not what she wanted but it was all she got. So she waited, she traded today. . . for tomorrow. When retirement came, he was a man of his word and she picked the unit, and off they headed on their grand adventure. Considering not only the enormous financial investment, but all the experiences and memories they gave up to buy this RV this trip had to be epic, and for her it was a trip she will never forget. Mere days later, somewhere just East of Phoenix Arizona he had a massive heart attack and died. Devastated, and numb she flew back to Ohio and had the RV towed home and put into storage where it sat for the next 10 years.

Selling the RV would be to admit that it was all a mistake for which there was no remedy.

That spring she finally asked her friend, the owner of the storage lot to pull the RV out of storage, clean it up and sell it. Like this couple who waited, hoped for and spent their lives for tomorrow, the number of people who waste their lives waiting, trading the reality of today for the mirage of tomorrow is heartbreaking.

"Therefore I say to you, do not worry about your life, what you will eat or what you will drink; nor about your body, what you will put on. Is not life more than food and the body more than clothing? Look at the birds of the air, for they neither sow nor reap nor gather into barns; yet your heavenly Father feeds them. Are you not of more value than they? Which of you by worrying can add one cubit to his stature? "So why do you worry about clothing? Consider the lilies of the field, how they grow: they neither toil nor spin; and yet I say to you that even Solomon in all his glory was not arrayed like one of these. Now if God so clothes the grass of the field, which today is, and tomorrow is thrown into the oven, will He not much more clothe you, O you of little faith? "Therefore, do not worry, saying, 'What shall we eat?' or 'What shall we drink?' or 'What shall we wear?' For after all these things the Gentiles seek. For your heavenly Father knows that you need all these things. But seek first the kingdom of God and His righteousness, and all these things shall be added to you. Therefore do not worry about tomorrow, for tomorrow will worry about its own things. Sufficient for the day is its own trouble."

— Matthew 6:25-34, NKJV

How am I going to handle this? . . . What am I going to do about that? . . . What if? . . . How many? . . .I am not ready . . . These are all the beginning of us trying to break the barrier of today into tomorrow and fix it before it gets to us. Untold billions have tried, and all have failed. This must be one of our adversary's favorite ploys. To get us to focus on a carrot we will never reach. To invest our passions in a day that is absent of God. God is the Great I Am, not the great I will be. He is in today, not tomorrow. Let me ask you a question, if we can't trust God with tomorrow, how do we find the faith to trust Him with our eternity?

An inappropriate concern for tomorrow is fear based.

Fear is a temptation that needs to be resisted like every other sin.

The truth is that worry and fear have creative ability. "For the thing I greatly feared has come upon me, and what I dreaded has happened to me."

— JOB 3:25, NKJV

What Job was saying is that the exact thing he was afraid of is what happened. For THE THING I greatly feared. This was no general fear that something bad was going to happen, it was extremely specific. THE THING. And it happened exactly like he feared. Job so greatly feared that one day (tomorrow) tragedy would strike the homes of his sons, that he would rise early and sacrifice to God just in case there was hidden sin in his grown children. His fear caused him to sacrifice even when there was no need to do so. Worse he took on responsibility for actions that these grown sons should have been doing for themselves. He tried to take a responsibility that belonged to someone else. The head of each household had been directed by God to offer sacrifices for their own home.

The very thing Job hoped to prevent from happening he released it to happen by his fear.

The story of Job is not the story of a sick one-upmanship between God and Satan with Job a mere inconsequential pawn. The gateway of fear that Job possessed was what Satan used to demand from God the right to attack Job. Satan used the permission slip of fear Job had given him. It's what he always uses. Let's put it this way: but without fear it is impossible to please Satan. They that come to him must believe that he is (by responding to fear) and that he is a rewarder of them that diligently fear him.

As embarrassing as this story is to tell, here goes.

I was alone late one night at the church and was so deeply involved in prayer and preparation for the next morning's service that I failed to notice that a storm was blowing in. The creeping and groaning of the old building alerted me that I needed to head home. The church building was poorly laid out and required one to turn off all the lights and then walk completely through the dark building to exit the front door. In the darkness with the howling wind and creaks everywhere I allowed my fear to take off running, which by the way was exactly what I did.

After exiting the building and locking the front door I ran up the sidewalk towards my car but when I got to the corner of the building somebody huge jumped out and attacked me. I have never had any martial arts training, but I was able to find my inner ninja and fight back. In a matter of seconds I was able kick my "attacker" twice and grab his arms and twist them until they snapped. It was then that I was able to look directly into the face of my attacker with his leaves and now broken branches. It seems the wind had moved the once attractive bush to attack me right as I rounded the corner. I cannot begin to describe to you my embarrassment the next morning as one person after another entered the church and asked what had happened to the formerly beautiful bush out front. My fear had taken a simple bush and made an assailant out of it. Fear has an uncanny ability to make us look stupid. Come to think about it I never did tell anyone at the church what happened. I hope they don't buy my book!

Fear is the substance of things worried about; the evidence of things not seen.

Faith is the currency of Heaven; fear is the currency of hell. Be careful where you invest.

Mark Twain is quoted as saying " I am now an old man and have known a great many troubles, most of which never happened." Fear at its core is simply not believing God. Or worse, believing Satan more.

What is the missing truth that causes all fear?

We think the devil hates us more than we know how much God loves us.

Because a perfect understanding of God's love for us casts out all fear. And when the enemy can convince us that God does not love us enough to take care of tomorrow, then we become our own god and try to handle it. As a mere human we are confined to today but as a god we are the same yesterday, today and forever and can affect tomorrow. Of course, that is sheer stupidity. We are human and we are confined to today. When we shove God aside and attempt to take over responsibility for tomorrow it is a pride issue straight from the one who is so full of pride he thinks he deserves to be worshipped.

The second day that will ruin your life is yesterday.

Did Jesus statement that He was anointed to "set at liberty them that are bruised" ever catch your attention? We often hear this verse or quote it ourselves, but have you ever meditated on it?

How does a bruise cause someone to need be set free?

It is reasonable to feel that someone who is bruised would need healed or comforted, or protected from further harm. But Jesus didn't say in this statement that He was purposed for any of that, he is empowered to set them free. Where is the connection between a bruise and imprisonment?

Yesterday.

Every bruise be it physical, emotional, or spiritual is the result of something that happened in our past. A bruise is not a surface wound, it is deeper and often does not show up until sometime after the injury. I have had bruises that I didn't know I had until later when I touched the spot where I was bruised. Contrary to what some people think, a bruise is not a sign of healing but is indication of a wound. Something has been broken and the normal flow of blood has been disrupted and there is pain where there should not be any.

Like a physical bruise, an emotional or spiritual bruise goes deep. They are the result of a traumatic event that disrupted the normal flow of life and when touched we respond to the pain by being angry, withdrawn, untrusting, cold, defensive, depressed, fearful, critical, judgmental, or driven. The bondage is manifest in addictions of innumerable measure. Some seek solace in alcohol, drugs, self-indulgence, but others in more subtle ways like over-eating, perfectionism, gossiping, materialism, hoarding, or overindulgence in sports, TV, gaming, physical appearance, fitness, or sex. Some are in bondage to drama; they almost seem allergic to living in peace seeing they repeatedly create circumstances that cause unrest and strife.

To society, some of these seem acceptable or honorable even but below the surface there is a bruise that is causing a person to be in bondage to it.

The tragedy is not what we are in bondage to but that we are in bondage at all.

Christ has made us free, totally free. We should be in bondage to nothing or nobody but Him.

We remain in bondage to any offense done to us or by us if we fail to fully forgive.

Whatever sins we retain they are retained; whatever sins we release they are released.

(See John 20:23)

To be free of an offense you must forgive them, you must forgive yourself, today.

Scripture tells us there is a special judgement awaiting those demonic spirits who left their first estate. Our first and only estate is today. This is the day the Lord has made, not that was the day or that will be the day, this is the day. God made today; He gave us today. For our own sake we need to find our comfort and joy in today, not yesterday or tomorrow. The choice is ours, we can give up the frustration of re-living yesterday and trying to fix tomorrow before it gets here or we can embrace the freedom that comes with letting go of yesterday, and trusting God with tomorrow while enjoying the right now moment we have.

Right now my friend, I come into agreement with you and we come into agreement with this truth.

Holy Spirit of God I know that you earnestly wait to bring comfort to the one reading this.

I declare that it is not by their might, it is not by their power, it is by you that they will have the strength to forgive. Regardless if the stones they hold are for themselves or intended for another, we drop them right now. This is over. Their past will no longer have a future, this ends today. Right now, totally. Bring healing to the hurt, bring freedom to the bruise. Free them. Remove the claim that darkness has had on their heart. They come to you wearied, they leave with joy unspeakable. We break off all lies, we declare an end to all voices not in agreement with yours. You are free in Jesus name!

4

IT'S NOT ABOUT YOU

If we're honest we will admit that us humans can become quite selfish at times. In fact, if left unchecked we can think that everything is about us. We see our world through that lens, and make every decision based on how it affects us. We also then bring that attitude into our relationship with God the Father. And that is where we have a crash landing. Jesus, while speaking of himself said that if you fall upon the rock you will be broken if the rock falls on you, you will be crushed. The reality is our choice is we are either crushed or broken.

When we get to the place that we think that our relationship with God is measured by what we have done or what we are experiencing it's time we learn a new truth.

In Luke chapter 15 we have a parable that Jesus shares with us that is come to be known as the parable of the prodigal son. We have totally hijacked that parable. It's not about the son, it's about the love of a father.

It's not about us.

In that chapter we come across this verse

"And not many days after, the younger son gathered all together, journeyed to a far country, and there wasted his possessions with prodigal living."

— Luke 15:13, NKJV

Not here, in fact nowhere in the parable is there a mention of a prodigal son. There is a son with prodigal living.

How you hear that changes everything.

Because in Abba Father's eyes, you are not what you do.

You are not an alcoholic, you are not a drug addict, you are not a sex addict, you are not a failed parent or a failed spouse, you are either a son or a daughter of God. You are a son or a daughter of God who does not yet know how good your heavenly father is and he so wants to show you.

The younger son wasted his life with prodigal living, and the older son wasted his life trying to serve his dad. At the end of the parable when the father is confronting the older son about his attitude towards his younger brother, the older son says that he has been serving his father these many years and has never transgressed any of his commandments at any time and yet the father never gave him a young goat that he might make merry with his friends.

Take this truth and bury it deep down into your spirit, you cannot earn from the father what he wants to freely give you. And until you know that. You are in a bondage called religion.

When Jesus was 12 years old, he got separated from his parents, and when they were reunited, he told his parents saying did you not know that I must be about my Father's business?

Do you know how impressed God the father was with that statement? God the Father was so impressed that we don't hear from Jesus for 18 years!

What 12-year-old Jesus did not understand was God the father is not looking for employees he is looking for sons and daughters.

18 years later Jesus rose out of the water of the Jordan river to hear the Father say this is my beloved son. Jesus was then driven by the Spirit of God into the wilderness to be tested to find out if he really knew that

he was a beloved son of God? Do you have any idea how much the Father loves you?

When you and I try to do something to earn favor with God, we display we really don't know how good he is. Because our relationship with him is not about us it's all about him.

He doesn't do for you because of how good you are, He does for you because of how good he is. You and I will not make it into heaven because of how good we are, we will make it into heaven because we believe in how good he is.

Let me pray for you right now, heavenly father I come to you and I declare freedom for the one reading these words. You have sent Jesus that we might know him and by knowing him we will be free. Because he that the son sets free is absolutely and completely free. And even though I am praying this now and they're reading it later your spirit and your words never returns void. I declare the power of your word and your spirit to set your people free. AMEN!

5

____

WHAT BATTLE ARE YOU RUNNING FROM?

For each of us there are some things that we are responsible for that we just don't like doing.

Until we bought a zero-turn lawnmower, I hated cutting grass. I could not think of anything that I would like to do less than cut grass. The two most beautiful sites I have ever seen was my wife coming down the aisle to join with me in marriage and the second was seeing our oldest son being able to push the lawnmower.

Truth is, even after all these years of serving God, there is still part of me that rebels when I _have_ to do something.

I will try to find a way out, I will try to get somebody else to do it for me, I will whine and complain until the last possible moment and then I will get it done. You know what I mean, like the night before the day taxes are due.

Several years ago, before it became common to file your taxes online, I found myself walking up to the post office box at 10 minutes before midnight on April 14th to drop my tax payment off. I ran into some guy I had never met before who was there for the same reason and we chatted with each other about waiting till the last moment before filing taxes. We both agreed this was a horrible idea and committed to each other we would never do it this late again. Next year, on April 14 minutes before midnight as I walked up to the same post office box to mail my tax return, I heard somebody mere feet away start laughing. As I looked up, I saw the same guy from a year earlier mailing his taxes!

In life, rarely does it pay to wait to the last moment and worse it can be tragic when we do not do what we're supposed to do.

The battle you are running from may have been sent to save you.

"It happened in the spring of the year, at the time when kings go out to battle, that David sent Joab and his servants with him, and all Israel; and they destroyed the people of Ammon and besieged Rabbah. But David remained at Jerusalem. Then it happened one evening that David arose from his bed and walked on the roof of the king's house. And from the roof he saw a woman bathing, and the woman was very beautiful to behold. So David sent and inquired about the woman.

— II SAMUEL 11:1-3

Did you catch that phrase, "the time when kings go off to war"?

The Bible says there is a time, a season for everything.

But do you know when we miss the season it changes who we are?

David missed the season when kings go off to war and he became an adulterer and murderer.

It's been said that the opportunity of a lifetime must be seized during the lifetime of the opportunity. When David lost the battle with his self-control by running from the battle that he faced, he initiated a battle with his eyes and his heart because he wasn't in the battle he was made for. Galatians 6:9 says let us not be weary in well doing for in due season we shall reap if we faint not.

Don't faint. Don't run from the battle that you have been equipped for because you will find yourself in a battle where you will be tempted above your ability to resist. Do not run *from* battle run *to* battle.

6

———

THE TRAGEDY OF AN UNKNOWN FATHER

My father came into a relationship with God just days before his passing. Before then his alcohol and anger issues greatly affected the man that he was. We could have had so much more. But in truth, he didn't know me, and I didn't understand him.

Because of the many years of abuse at the hands of my earthly father, I found it difficult to connect with God the Father. I wrongly assumed my deep connection with Jesus and the Holy Spirit was enough. I had no idea what I was missing!

For the first few years I was a believer I hated hearing or reading John 3:16. For God so loved the world that he gave his only begotten son . . . When I read or heard that verse I saw my heavy set father, drunk, sitting in his recliner barking out orders to his sons. We were doing the work because I figured he was too lazy to do it himself. When I thought about my heavenly father, I projected onto him that he was like my earthly father, so he sent his son to die for us instead of doing it himself.

I know, that hurts me even now to type those words, but prolonged pain has a way of twisting our thinking in knots. Is there pain from your relationship with someone that is twisting your perception of truth?

One day God saw fit to bless my wife and I with our first child.

When he was just a few months old he woke in the middle of the night crying to be fed and I volunteered to let my wife sleep as I fed him. As we sat in the rocking chair there was enough moonlight coming through the window that I didn't need to turn on the room light to take care of the feeding.

As this beautiful child, our child, with his face bathed in moonlight drank from his bottle his tiny hand reached up and wrapped itself around my little finger. I was in awe of how tiny and delicate his little fingers were. He was making little noises as he ate letting me know he was thoroughly enjoying himself. As I gently rocked back and forth, and my eyes filled with tears at the wonder of God and his creation, God the father spoke to me. "If an angry mob was pounding on your door demanding that someone in your home must be brutally sacrificed for the sins of the mob, could you love them enough to send your son?" As the abject horror of that thought flooded my heart and then my eyes with emotion, God said to me "I did".

Like a floodgate had opened I poured my heart out and repented of the horrible attitude I had held towards him for years. My eyes were like fountains and I struggled to clear them so I could get a look to see that our son was ok. For some reason in that moment I felt like he was vulnerable, likely brought on by the very thought of having to give him up for someone else's failure. As I was able to compose myself God had a request. He simply said, "I would appreciate it if you would quit viewing seeing me as fat and lazy".

I do not know how to describe the emotion that came with his words except to say that this was not a rebuke, it was as if my thoughts, my words, had hurt him.

This was the beginning of my journey to come to know the immeasurable love that Father God has for us and more than that, what that knowledge does to free us.

In Luke 15 is a parable that has come to be known as The Parable of the Prodigal Son. Please consider taking a moment and read it again before moving forward.

"Then He said: "A certain man had two sons. And the younger of them said to his father, 'Father, give me the portion of goods that falls to me. ' So he divided to them his livelihood. And not many days after, the younger son gathered all together, journeyed to a far country, and there wasted his possessions with prodigal living. But when he had spent all, there arose a severe famine in that land, and he began to be in want. Then he went and joined himself to a citizen of that country, and he sent him into his fields to feed swine. And he would gladly have filled his stomach with the pods that the swine ate, and no one gave him anything. "But when he came to himself, he said, 'How many of my father's hired servants have bread enough and to spare, and I perish with hunger! I will arise and go to my father, and will say to him, "Father, I have sinned against heaven and before you, and I am no longer worthy to be called your son. Make me like one of your hired servants."' "And he arose and came to his father. But when he was still a great way off, his father saw him and had compassion, and ran and fell on his neck and kissed him. And the son said to him, 'Father, I have sinned against heaven and in your sight, and am no longer worthy to be called your son.' "But the father said to his servants, 'Bring out the best robe and put it on him, and put a ring on his hand and sandals on his feet. And bring the fatted calf here and kill it, and let us eat and be merry; for this my son was dead and is alive again; he was lost and is found.' And they began to be merry. "Now his older son was in the field. And as he came and drew near to the house, he heard music and dancing. So he called one of the servants and asked what these things meant. And he said to him, 'Your brother has come, and because he has received him safe and sound, your father has killed the fatted calf.' "But he was angry and would not go in. Therefore his father came out and pleaded with him. So he answered and said to his father, 'Lo, these many years I have been serving you; I never transgressed your commandment at any time; and yet you never gave me a young goat, that I might make merry with my friends. But as soon as this son of yours came, who has devoured your livelihood with harlots, you killed the fatted calf for him.'

"And he said to him, 'Son, you are always with me, and all that I have is yours. It was right that we should make merry and be glad, for your brother was dead and is alive again, and was lost and is found.'

— Luke 15:11-32, NKJV

Jesus started this parable by saying "There was a certain man who had two sons".

This entire parable was meant to convey a truth to us about a certain man. Jesus is always very clear as he communicates with us and he started this parable doing what all great communicators do, telling us what they're talking about. A certain man. And this man had two sons, so the certain man is a father. Since we know that Jesus came to reveal the heart of the father to us, we know that the certain man, this father, depicts the heart and the attitude of our heavenly Father.

If we want to align ourselves with the heart of Jesus in this parable, we should know that this is a parable about a father. A very very good father.

The greatest truths of this parable are not fully known until we read it as a parable about a father and not a parable of a prodigal son, whatever that is.

Let's be clear, what God wants you to know, regardless of what you face, regardless of what you feel, regardless of what you've been told, the greatest need you have is to know how good your heavenly Father is and that He is deeply in love with your heart.

In the parable both of these sons had a relationship with dad, but neither of them knew their dad. I suspect that describes where many of us are at. Let's see what the next few minutes of reading reveal to us

---

"And not many days after, **the younger son** gathered all together, journeyed to a far country, and there wasted his possessions with **prodigal living."**

— LUKE 15:13, NKJV

In the Father's eyes you are not what you do.

Notice that Jesus in this parable did not describe any son as being a prodigal son. He simply described him as the younger son. In the beginning of the parable he's the younger son, when he's in the middle of his mess he's the younger son, at the end of the story he's the younger son. He never was anything but a son.

For too long we have attached to ourselves labels based on what we do or what others have said about us. There comes a change in our perspective when we grasp the reality that our heavenly Father does not describe us by what we do but by who we are. Regardless of what we do or have done.

He was not a prodigal son. He was a son in prodigal living. What he did, did not change who he was. You and I did not become a child of God by anything we have done. We became His child by what he has done.

What you have done has not changed who you are. God will not engage us on our misconceptions of who we are, He will engage us on the basis of who He knows us to be, and what He hopes we will do. He is always looking forward.

You are not a prodigal, an addict, a failure, a disappointment, or any of the other countless words you may use to describe yourself. You are his son. You are his daughter. Everything else is secondary.

Your struggles are because you are a child who doesn't know how really really good your Heavenly Father is and he is earnest in desiring to change that.

"But when he came to himself, he said, 'How many of my father's hired servants have bread enough and to spare, and I perish with hunger!"

— Luke 15:17, NKJV

Read that verse again because you're going to be surprised that you missed the greatest truth in this verse. It says when he came to himself, he began to talk about his father. There are many believers today who are wasting their life trying to find themselves. You cannot truly find yourself until you get to know your heavenly father. This son found himself when he came to the realization of how good his father was. My dad treats his servants better than I am treating myself he said. You will find yourself, when you find him. When you come to the understanding that your heavenly father is beyond your wildest imagination good. And you are his son or daughter. That truth nullifies every lie that has been spoken over your life. Your heavenly father is very very good and you are his child. Knowing that, changes everything, knowing that changes you.

"Then he went and joined himself to a citizen of that country, and he sent him into his fields to feed swine. And he would gladly have filled his stomach with the pods that the swine ate, and no one gave him anything."

— Luke 15:15-16, NKJV

When you join yourself to anything outside the Father's kingdom you become a servant to it.

You are struggling right now, you are hurting right now because you have joined yourself to the wrong people in the wrong kingdom. Quit selling yourself to acquire that which your Heavenly Father never intended for you to have.

When we allow other people to treat us in a manner that is unlike how our heavenly father would treat us, their lie becomes our truth. They believe a lie about you and treat you accordingly. If you allow it, that becomes your reality.

The younger son is not the only one trapped by this deception.

"So he answered and said to his father, 'Lo, these many years I have been serving you; I never **transgressed your commandements** at any time; and yet you never gave me a young goat, that I might make merry with my friends."

— LUKE 15:29, NKJV

How did the older son get to the place that his relationship with dad is summed up in "I have kept all your commandments"? A better question is, how did *you* get there? If you think that a relationship with God is simply keeping all his commandments you are in bondage to religion.

Of course, we should keep his commandments, but we do that out of love, not to gain something. What pain it must have caused the father when he realized that all this time his son has been working to *gain* what the father was eagerly willing to *give*. The son didn't know that because he was too busy being a servant instead of being a son.

The father's response could be paraphrased like this. Why are you slaving away to gain that which I have already given you? I am your dad, you are my child, everything I have is yours. You don't get everything I have because of how good you are, you get everything I have because of how good I am.

Jesus could so relate to this older son. The scripture tells us that Jesus learned obedience. That means Jesus wasn't born knowing everything, just like you and I he needed to learn it. He needed to learn his proper relationship on this earth with his Father.

Do you remember the time when Jesus was 12 years old and he got left behind by the caravan? Do you remember his response? When questioned by his parents he responded by asking "did you not know I needed to be about my father's business?" That may seem noble, that may even seem to be the right attitude, but if we want to know what our Heavenly Father thinks about it, we see that we don't hear from Jesus for 18 years! So much for being about Father's business.

18 years later Jesus walks to the edge of a river where he is then baptized by John the Baptist. When he comes out of the river the Spirit of God in the form of a dove settles on Him and a voice from heaven says "this is my beloved servant son in whom I am very pleased".

We have no record of Jesus doing any *business* for 18 years and yet the Father was pleased with him. You need to know that God the Father has the ability to be pleased with you even if you have done nothing good.

Immediately, the Bible says, the Spirit of God drove Jesus into the wilderness to be tempted. What was he tempted with? He was tempted concerning this one simple truth, is he the Son of God? Because at the end of it all, that's the only truth that matters. THAT is the truth our adversary would like to steal from us.

God is not looking for employees, He is wanting sons and daughters.

"But when he came to himself, he said, 'How many of my father's hired servants have bread enough and to spare, and I perish with hunger! **I will arise and go to my father,** and will say to him, "Father, I have sinned against heaven and before you,"

— LUKE 15:17-18, NKJV

To repent is to arise

Penthouse is understood to mean the top floor, the best.

Pent-house. The top floor of the house.

Re means to do again as in repeat.

Re-pent means to put yourself back on top.

The Word of God guides us on how to get back on top of life and it's issues, repent. More than a command, it is an incredible gift.

I want to encourage you to do something radical here. I want you to begin to talk to God and tell him that you truly want to know how good he is and how much he loves you. Ask him to reveal himself to you in ways he never has before. And then believe.

I would encourage you to read the gospel of John through several times.

The entirety of the word of God is divinely inspired and holds great truth for us. But the apostle John had a relationship with God like no one else. The Bible itself calls him the disciple whom Jesus loved. We know that Jesus loves everyone, so the Bible is not saying that John is the only disciple loved but rather John knew better than all the other disciples how loved he was. The Spirit of God wants you to know it also.

No matter how far you have gone or what you have done God is still your Father

When the younger son was living with dad and content to live with dad, dad was his dad. When the younger son was no longer satisfied with living with dad and selfishly took everything he could and left, dad was still dad. When the younger son wasted his life and everything dad had given him, dad was still dad. At no time during this entire parable was dad anything other than dad and the sons anything other than a son.

The lack of a full understanding of this truth has caused the church to act goofy.

Which is it, once saved always saved or born again, and again, and again, and again?

The truth is it's neither.

The fact that we are even asking the question shows we really don't understand how things work with father God.

In the beginning of the parable both sons had a relationship with dad and they had fellowship with dad.

But when dad gave the inheritance to both of the sons that gift caused the younger son to lose fellowship with dad. It would help if you understood this, father God greatly desires fellowship with you. God knows that if he gives you everything you asked for it may cause you to lose fellowship with him. That is not a trade he's willing to make. That very thing that has caused you to be angry with God because you never received it may be the very thing that will cause you to lose fellowship with God and that's why he has not yet given it to you. I say yet because he loves to give and he will withhold no good gift from you. A gift that separates you from his fellowship is not a good gift. When your relationship with him becomes so deep and so rooted that there is nothing that can separate you from God then he will withhold no good thing from you. God will never bless you out of fellowship with him. Maybe just maybe you didn't get that promotion because the challenges could cause you to lose fellowship with God. Maybe just maybe you didn't get that relationship you desired because that relationship will cause you to lose fellowship with God. And he's so values his fellowship with you. Maybe just maybe when you get to the place that nothing will withhold your fellowship with God then God is freed to withhold no good thing from you.

We are often confused about our standing with God because we don't understand the difference between relationship and fellowship. The sons lost fellowship with their father but they never lost relationship.

Some say if you have no fellowship with God you have lost relationship. There is no basis for truth in that statement. They are suggesting that when I need God the most he has abandoned me. As if God were that fickle.

He even suggested in Scripture that it would be easier for a mother to forget that the child she is nursing at her breast is her child, than for him to forget that we are his daughter or son. He has carved us in the palm of his hands.

There is a reason that God has all of us believers here. We are all called to be witnesses. A witness shares with others what he or she has seen or experienced. We are called to share with others just how very good our Heavenly Father is. We are to share of his incredible love for all of mankind and his desire to meet all of our needs according to his riches in glory. It's called living in the kingdom. It is the will of God that we have a foretaste of what heaven is like while we live down here. That's why he instructed us to pray that His kingdom come and his will be done in earth as it is in heaven. That's why Jesus himself said the kingdom of God is at hand. We cannot be a true witness if we have not experienced what it's like to be loved by God. For too many in the church they have become lawyers instead of witnesses. They just want to argue with the unbelieving. They just want argue with the lost. We have not been called to be lawyers we are called to be witnesses.

This is the reason why the church where we pastor does not hold any fundraisers. Doing so would make us poor witnesses. How do we witness to a community of the incredible love, mercy and glory of God when we have had to beg from that same community just to pay our bills?

That's also why we spend very little time in a church service receiving the offering. Typically, it's mere moments.

God's goal is to get you into heaven but he is not in a hurry to do it.

He wants to use you as a witness about how good he is.

If you are living in a pig pen that is not what God has for you and you will not be a good witness.

There are too many in the church today who have gotten saved and that's a relationship with God, and they have no idea what it means to fellowship with him.

When we place our full confidence in what Jesus did we gain access to the relationship and fellowship he had with the Father

---

"But when he came to himself, he said, 'How many of my father's hired servants have bread enough and to spare, and I perish with hunger! I will arise and go to my father, and will say to him, "Father, I have sinned against heaven and before you, and I am no longer worthy to be called your son. Make me like one of your hired servants." ' "And he arose and came to his father.

— Luke 15:17-20, NKJV

Change the root. The root determines the fruit

We have to quit focusing on trying to stop sinning.

We have to find the root to our sin. I sincerely believe that root is we don't know how good your heavenly father is. Remember, the younger son came to himself not when he realized how bad he was but when he realized how good his father was. That's what motivated the change in his attitude and his actions. For too long we in the church have been swimming against the tide. We have been trying to teach sinners how not to sin.

It's like putting lipstick on a pig. And we end up with a church house full of pigs with lipstick on but nobody's heart has been changed.

And without a heart change nothing will ever change. We have taught people how to hide their sin, we have taught them how to be hypocrites, it's time that we teach them how to be sons and daughters. We have not been called to the business of pointing out other people's sins. We have been called to be witnesses of how good our heavenly father is. Nobody runs to the father based on how bad they are, we run to the father when we know how good he is. We love Him because we came to know he first loved us.

Never elevate the strength of your sin above the love of the Father.

"And the son said to him, 'Father, I have sinned against heaven and in your sight, and am no longer worthy to be called your son.' "But the father said to his servants,

— Luke 15:21-22, NKJV

Did you catch that? The younger son had practiced the speech he was going to give his dad when he arrived home. All the way from the pigpen to the porch he ran the words over and over in his head. Father I am not worthy to be your son. And dad never let him finish the speech.

If you want God to ignore you, try telling Him how unworthy you are.

When you talk about how unworthy you are you are focusing on the wrong thing. Your father already knows how unworthy you are, that's not what is important, it's about how good he is.

When in the parable did the Father forgive the son?

Was it when the son left with all of his goods? Was it when the son decided to return home? Was it when the son arrived back home?

The parable never tells us because forgiveness wasn't needed. Repentance was needed, forgiveness wasn't.

When you were born again all things become new. In that moment your Heavenly Father forgave you not only of every sin you ever committed but every sin you would ever commit. That frees him to treat you and I as if we had never sinned. It's called justification. When we repent we tap into that forgiveness. God is not waiting to forgive you, he's waiting for you to repent. He has already forgiven you. That's why you don't get born again and again and again. What is it that can separate you from the love of the father? Paul said he was persuaded that nothing could separate him from the love of the father. Some reading this book have fallen for the deception that their sin is greater than God's ability to forgive. That's just not true. If you have an ability that is greater than God's ability that makes you God. Newsflash, you're not God.

Forgiveness wasn't needed. father was just happy the son figured out how good dad was so father could start celebrating. If you are a parent and you were reading this did you throw your child away the first time they messed their diaper? The second time? The third time? If you and I with our fallen nature have the ability to love beyond the mess how much more our Heavenly Father?

Just now as I was preparing to write the next portion of this chapter the Holy Spirit moved my heart and had me stop right now and pray for somebody who is going to be reading this book. That person may be you. You feel so all alone right now and your life feels like it's such a mess and you really have lost all hope that life will ever make sense again, if it ever did. I want to tell you that you're Heavenly Father knows exactly who you are and what you're going through and he is maneuvering things in your life to bring peace into your pain. It has already begun.

Asking for forgiveness doesn't change God's mind about you. It changes your mind about you.

It is shocking sometimes how little we in the church understand forgiveness. The Holy Spirit wants to clear that up. Forgive is actually a compound word made up of two words, fore and give.

When we give some thing it's not a payment and it's not in response to the actions of another person. It's an act out of our heart. True giving happens when our love for another individual is so compelling that we want to go beyond mere words, we want to do something for them. We want to add something to their life that makes their life better. That's where the heart of God is. He's so loved the world that he gave. That giving wasn't a reflection of the character of the world it was a reflection of the character of our Heavenly Father . He is so good that he gave to those who didn't deserve it. The second word is fore. It means beforehand or at the beginning. When you put the two words together you get forgive. That tells us that when God forgives us he gives us a release from our sin before we even ask. He fore gives.

Most people think God's forgiveness is like a credit card. But the truth is God's forgiveness is like a debit card. When there is a credit card there is a debt that is owed. With a debit card the debt has already been paid, we are simply making a withdrawal. When Jesus hung on the cross and he cried out it is finished, at that moment all the sins of the entire world from the beginning to the end were paid for. Every human ever to exist was fully forgiven.

God is not waiting for us to ask him for forgiveness he already gave us forgiveness for everything we've ever committed or will commit. When we repent we receive the benefit of that forgiveness. When Scripture says that old things have passed away and all things have become new, it meant all old things and all things became new. All things.

""But when he came to himself, he said, 'How many of my father's hired servants have bread enough and to spare, and I perish with hunger! I will arise and go to my father . . .

— Luke 15:17-18, NKJV

Forgiveness doesn't move God toward you, it moves you toward God. For too long the church has talked about a angry vindictive God that shut us off every time we make a mistake. We have taught that when we sin he doesn't want to talk to us, when we sin he can't wait to exact punishment. That is not who God is. All of that anger for our sin, all of the need of a holy God for justice was poured out on Jesus as he hung on the cross. That debt has been fully paid. He does not abandon us when we sin. What kind of a father would he be if he left us when we needed him the most? As he looked down at the woman caught in the act of adultery and said to her neither do I condemn you go and sin no more, we need to understand something. His words are spirit and they are life. When he spoke to that broken daughter of his he was not instructing her to go and sin no more, his love through his words were ***empowering*** her to go and sin no more.

Noticed what he didn't say, he never said I forgive you. From his words it is crystal clear he had already forgiven her. He did not look on her with anger or disappointment and neither does he look at you that way. He looked at her with compassion. When everybody else had abandoned her, even the man she was just in bed with, and everybody saw her as a failure Jesus came alongside of her, having no compulsion to condemn her he spoke life into her heart. My dear brother, my dear sister, I want you to know, that is exactly what he desires to do for you. No matter what has dragged you into your predicament, God stands ready to come alongside of you and speak life into you. Forgiveness does not change what God thinks about you, it changes what you think about you. Never forget that while you and I were sinners God sent his son to die for us. When we were at our worst he sent his best. That tells you everything you need to know about your father's love for you.

In our parable this younger son changed his mind about himself when he thought about how good his father was.

That realization brought him back to dad, it did not bring dad back to him.

God has more for you than you have wasted.

""But when he came to himself, he said, 'How many of my father's hired servants have bread enough and to spare, and I

> perish with hunger! I will arise and go to my father, and will say to him, "Father, I have sinned against heaven and before you, and I am no longer worthy to be called your son. Make me like one of your hired servants."
>
> — Luke 15:17-19, NKJV

This son fully expected to come home to dad and be some kind of second-class citizen in dad's kingdom. He really didn't know his father. There was no way dad was going let him be like just one of the hired servants.

He was a son, he was always a son.

God does not supply all of your needs according to how good you've been it's according to his riches in glory. It's about how good he is. The father's plan was to do exceeding abundantly above all that the son could ask or think. Dad gave him a robe, a ring, and sandals.

The robe represented righteousness. It identified him as a member of the family.

We substantially financially support an orphanage in a Third World country. In talking to the directors of that country I asked them to walk me through the process of them taking in an orphan child. They told me the first thing they do is give them a T-shirt with the name of the orphanage in big letters on the front of the shirt. I asked them why they did that and their response blew me away. In their country there is many orphan children that are abandoned on the streets. They are left to themselves define food and shelter wherever they can. Those children who do not belong to anybody often go missing. Bad things happen to them because they are viewed as not belonging to anybody. But when they put the T-shirt on the child if not only says something to the child, it says something to the rest of the world. This is not an orphan child. This child belongs, and somebody is looking after them. When you and I repent God is fitting us with a robe that we can't see with a natural eye but to the spiritual realm it speaks that we belong and somebody's looking after us.

The ring was used as a symbol of authority. That ring opens opportunities and could be used to acquire things.

The authority was not in the person, it was in the ring that they wore. Jesus tried to tell us that not even a sparrow falls to the ground without our having a father knowing it.

Every morning birds wake up while it is still dark and begin to sing. They are not worried about where they're going to find food, or who is going to provide for them, they just start their day with praise. Everything else takes care of itself as far as they are concerned. Wouldn't it be great if we could learn to live like that? We can, and we should.

The shoes represented peace. Dad wanted his son to walk in peace just like he wants you to walk in peace.

We do not fight for peace, we fight from peace. Our adversary is always trying to get us agitated and upset so we will engage him in the flesh. In the spirit we win, in the flesh we lose. We must stay in peace, we must stay in the spirit.

You have to get ahold of this truth, this son ended up with more than what he left with. Nothing you have done, no failure in your life has the ability to restrict what God is able to do for you, in you, and through you.

You have got talk yourself out of your mess.

"But when he came to himself, **he said**, 'How many of my father's hired servants have bread enough and to spare, and I perish with hunger! I will arise and go to my father, and **will say** to him, "Father, I have sinned against heaven and before you,"

— LUKE 15:17-18, NKJV

When the younger son was talking, he was not talking to the pigs nor was he talking to anybody else, he was talking to himself. Let me say this as gently as I can without diminishing the impact. Jesus once said do not cast your pearls before pigs. There may be some pigs in your life that you need to quit talking to. They do not have your best interest at heart, they are not going to help you. You are doing more than wasting your time, you are harming yourself because you are going to a cloud that has no rain, a well that has no water.

He was by himself when he came to himself and he said to himself, my father is good and he has a place for me.

The enemy has deceived some by getting them to believe they *are* a mess instead of being *in* a mess.

Please read that last sentence again.

You are gloriously and wonderfully made. You are a child of the most high God. You are not a mess. God doesn't make messes. God does not look on the outward, he looks at your heart. And he knows buried beneath all of that hurt, and all of that pain, all of that mess, is good. He knows because he put it there. And somewhere, because of something that was said, or something that was done you have believed a lie that you are a mess. Nothing could be further from the truth. You are a son or daughter of God who is in a mess. You need to stop talking to pigs and start speaking truth to yourself. The only thing you lack is knowing how so very much your heavenly father is in love with your heart. Jesus died to show you how good of a father he is.

When he came to himself

That was when he started to speak truth to himself.

When he started speaking truth to himself his situation quickly changed. Please catch that, his situation did not change so that he could speak truth to himself, he spoke truth to himself and his situation changed. We often do that backwards.

A pig will try to talk to you about how you got in this mess, what you did wrong, and what you need to start doing right to fix it. You see, if you are drowning, to your heavenly father it doesn't matter whether you are drowning because you jumped, fell or were pushed, he just doesn't want you drowning anymore. So he gave you the power of death and life, and it's in your tongue. Quit speaking death over your-self start speaking life. Truth is always life; truth will always set you free.

"And he would gladly have filled his stomach with the pods that the swine ate, and no one gave him anything."

— LUKE 15:16, NKJV

The pig pen was a place that reminded him of his failure

Some church people have caused churches to become pig pens by reminding people of their failures. You are not a pig, you should not be in a pigpen. Your father has prepared a place for you and he can't wait for you to know how good he is.

In the middle of this story we have these words about the younger son, "but when he came to himself". If you go back and read the parable again, it will jump off the page to you that he did not come to himself when he realized how bad he was, he came to himself when he realized how good his father was. Counting on the goodness of his father he prepared a speech wherein he tells his father i've sinned against you and I am not worthy to be called your son. And then he tries to tell dad how he should treat him, like one of the servants.

I can just imagine him practicing that speech over and over again on the long march back to dad's house. As he stood in front of dad he began his speech, and it's as if the father doesn't hear a single word of it, because dad never responds. The Scripture says, "but the father said to his servants".

If you understand what just took place the father ignored everything the son had to say and engage his servants to bring out the best robe, put a ring on his son's hand and sandals on his feet. The father in the story wasn't being rude, but he understands a great spiritual truth that evades most Christians.

Our value to the father is not determined by us it's determined by him.

And anything we say or feel or think that is contrary to the value he has placed upon us, he doesn't want to hear about it. He doesn't want to hear you repent again for something for which you have already repented. He doesn't want to hear you talk about how bad you are, what a failure, how you will never get it right.

So I get a sense he doesn't appreciate it when his kids try to tell him that they have no value.

His love for you makes you valuable.

Father is in a hurry to make it known to you and the entire universe that you are covered, that you have a place, and get you walking in peace. That is all he has ever wanted all along.

So, quit telling your heavenly father for the second or third or fourth or fifth time how sorry you are. Quit telling him how useless you feel, or what a failure you are. He will not believe you, because he is not listening. Just shut up and get dressed. Your father loves you more than you know. He is incredibly in love with your heart.

7

FOUR THINGS GOD WANTS YOU TO HEAR

"Now it came to pass in the days when the judges ruled, that there was a famine in the land. And a certain man of Beth–lehem–judah went to sojourn in the country of Moab, he, and his wife, and his two sons. And the name of the man was Elimelech, and the name of his wife Naomi, and the name of his two sons Mahlon and Chilion, Ephrathites of Beth–lehem–judah. And they came into the country of Moab, and continued there. And Elimelech Naomi's husband died; and she was left, and her two sons. And they took them wives of the women of Moab; the name of the one was Orpah, and the name of the other Ruth: and they dwelled there about ten years. And Mahlon and Chilion died also both of them; and the woman was left of her two sons and her husband. Then she arose with her daughters in law, that she might return from the country of Moab: for she had heard in the country of Moab how that the Lord had visited his people in giving them bread. Wherefore she went forth out of the place where she was, and her two daughters in law with her; and they went on the way to return unto the land of Judah. And Naomi said unto her two daughters in law, Go, return each to her mother's house: the Lord deal kindly with you, as ye have dealt with the dead, and with me. The Lord grant you that ye may find rest, each of you in the house of her husband. Then she kissed them; and they lifted up their voice, and wept. And they said unto her, Surely we will return with thee unto thy people. And Naomi said, Turn again, my daughters: why will ye go with me? are there yet any more sons in my womb, that they may be your husbands? Turn again, my daughters, go your way; for I am too old to have an husband. If I should say, I have hope, if I should have an husband also to night, and should also bear sons; Would ye tarry for them till they were grown? would ye stay for them from having husbands? nay, my daughters; for it grieveth me much for your sakes that the hand of the Lord is gone out against me. And they lifted up their voice, and wept again: and Orpah kissed her mother in law; but Ruth clave unto her. And she said, Behold, thy sister in law is gone back unto her people, and unto her gods: return thou after thy sister in law. And Ruth said, Entreat me not to leave thee, or to return from following after thee: for whither thou goest, I will go; and where thou lodgest, I will lodge: thy people shall be my people, and thy God my God: Where thou diest, will I die, and there will I be buried: the Lord do so to me, and more also, if ought but death part thee and me. When she saw that she was stedfastly minded to go with her, then she left speaking unto her. So they two went until they came to Beth–lehem. And it came to pass, when they were come to Beth–lehem, that all the city was moved about them, and they said, Is this Naomi? And she said unto them, Call me not Naomi, call me Mara: for the Almighty hath dealt very bitterly with me. I went out full, and the Lord hath brought me home again empty: why then call ye me Naomi, seeing the Lord hath testified against me, and the Almighty hath afflicted me? So Naomi returned, and Ruth the Moabitess, her daughter in law, with her, which returned out of the country of Moab: and they came to Beth–lehem in the beginning of barley harvest."

— RUTH 1:1-22, KJV

We cannot fully grasp the challenge that Naomi faced when tragedy struck and found her in a society that has no safety net.

But you are not reading this book to learn about somebody else's struggles, you have enough of your own.

If you are like me, as you go through struggles you not only wrestle with the voices in your head but you also have well-meaning people who want to offer advice.

And sometimes the best remedy is to shut out all the other voices and focus simply on the *one* voice that matters. What does God have to say about me right now?

I want to share with you four things you can be absolutely sure God would say to you in any moment of your life no matter what you've done, what you're going through, or what you face.

The first thing God would say to you is I know who you are.

Amid her pain Naomi lost sight of who she was. She began to ask others to call her Mara, which means bitterness. I think one of the most destructive things we do when we go through difficult times is we make the mistake of thinking that these difficult times define us. Nothing could be further from the truth. You are who God says you are. Your creator, your savior, your God knows exactly who you are. Nothing you have gone through, nothing you have done has changed how he sees you. God knows who you are. You have not gotten lost in a crowd, your identity has not been blurred, he has not set you aside. God chose you and he would choose you again.

God knows who you are and he knows that you are fearfully and wonderfully made. He formed you for a purpose. He knows the thoughts he has toward you and they are nothing but good. He has not given up on you, he has not left you or forsaken you, and he will not engage you based on your present circumstances. He knows who you are. He will always engage you from that perspective.

Don't invite him to your pity party because he won't attend. He has made you more than a conqueror, he has made you to sit in heavenly places with Christ Jesus. As you go through this season, as you face the struggle, know this, he will never lose sight of who you are. If you were in a stadium full of people, he could walk up to you, look you in the face and call you by your name and tell you, you are mine. As long as you are drawing breath nothing will change that.

I am talking to someone who doesn't know who they are.

God wants you to know that not even for a moment has he lost sight of who you are. When you get out of this season you are in you will still be you in his eyes

Secondly God would tell you I know how you feel.

One of the most destructive things that can happen to a human being is loneliness. It's the first thing declared by God to not be good. Loneliness destroys a person from the inside out. Everything else in life falls apart when we are lonely. Our adversary is a bully. He likes to separate us from all the sources of help and encouragement. One of his tools is to make us to believe that nobody understands, nobody knows how we feel.

God wants you to know this he is touched by your feelings of inadequacy. He has been tempted, through Jesus, in every way that you and I have ever faced. He knows how you feel. He wants you to know that because he wants you to know that you were not going through this alone.

Your hurts hurt him. Your pain pains him.

Regardless of how you have gotten into this mess he has no condemnation for you. He wants you to know he knows how you feel and that you are not alone. He said he would never leave you or for sake you and he absolutely meant that.

Thirdly he would tell you that no matter what has happened, no matter what you have done, I still have a will for your life.

There is a good chance that what you were struggling with right now is because of the actions of another human being. Maybe they said or did something or worse, maybe they have walked away. Those people who walked away were never meant to be a part of your destiny. If they can walk away, let them walk. If they walk away your destiny is not tied to them. God does not need what is gone, he will work with what is left.

The less the better. Think empty pots, an empty fishing vessel, a little boy's lunch.

Lastly, he would tell you I love you.

If you are reading this book I can tell you with absolute certainty that nothing you have done nor anything that is happened to you has separated you from the love that God has for you. He loves you, and there's nothing you can do about that but to accept it. He loves you. He always has. If God had a wallet your picture would be inside of it. You cannot even comprehend the full extent of his love for you. Please do not allow what others have done or said or your circumstances speaking to you to change your mind about how much your heavenly father loves you.

"And God will wipe away every tear from their eyes; there shall be no more death, nor sorrow, nor crying. There shall be no more pain, for the former things have passed away."

— REVELATION 21:4, NKJV

Sometime back the Holy Spirit brought this scripture to my mind and with it came a download of information. In that moment I understood this truth. He wipes every tear from our eyes by revealing to us when we are in heaven why we had to go through what we went through. With that information we will see and know what he saw and knows. There will no longer a reason to be sad because everything will have worked together for our good.

"I know that whatever God does, It shall be forever. Nothing can be added to it, And nothing taken from it. God does it, that men should fear before Him."

— ECCLESIASTES 3:14, NKJV

I understand the first part of that verse to mean that when you and I engage a problem, we just want the pain to go away. God engages our problems to solve them so that the pain is gone forever. When everything is said and done, we will see and understand what he now sees and understands. We will then say to him it's perfect, nothing can be added to it and nothing can be taken from it. We will be in awe at the love and wisdom by which our heavenly father engaged us and solved our hurt forever. Until then never ever doubt for a moment how so incredibly in love with you he is. You will get through this and you will be better because of it. Guaranteed.

8

IT'S TIME TO LEAVE

I f you felt led to read this chapter, if it's possible that the Holy Spirit brought you here, you probably need to move. You are likely living in the wrong neighborhood.

There is a spirit that has long roamed this planet. We see it pop its head up in the conversation between the serpent and Eve. We see the fruits of his efforts in the story of Cain and Able. This spirit invites you to move into its hood. Much like a demonic version of the song sung by the wholesome Mr. Rogers, it lures us with its perverted song.

It's a terrible day in this neighborhood,
A painful day for a neighbor,
Would you be mine?
Could you be mine?
It's a terrible day in this neighborhood,
A perfect day for some misery,
Would you be mine?
Could you be mine?
I have always wanted to have a neighbor just like you,
I have always wanted to live in a neighborhood with you.
So let's make the most of your pain today,

Since we're together, we might as well say,
Would you be mine?
Could you be mine?
Won't you be my neighbor?
Won't you please,
Won't you please,
Please won't you be my neighbor?

The cost of entry into this hood is universally available, it requires only that you have suffered some kind of loss or face some kind of battle. In this hood you can find camaraderie with other likeminded people. You will be lonely, but you will never be alone. There will always be somebody to talk to, there will always be somebody who knows how you feel, there will always be someone to pity you.

In this hood you will often find compassion, attention, even meaningful relationships. But this hood is so toxic it will kill you both spiritually and emotionally and can make you physically ill.

The name of this hood is victimhood.

Nobody in victimhood has joy.

Nobody in victimhood is ever cured.

Nobody in victimhood goes to heaven.

All the way back in the garden when the serpent opened its mouth and spoke to Eve, he introduced victimhood. He told Eve that God made her a victim by keeping something from her and she needed to fix that. Immediately she saw herself as a victim of God's actions and took it upon herself to change her situation and by doing so she moved into victimhood.

No human that has ever lived has lived a life free from pain. It's just part of the human experience of living in a fallen world. Yet you get to choose whether you allow that pain to define you. You get to choose if you are a victim or a victor.

Your adversary cannot manipulate you until he gets you to believing the lie that you are a victim.

The typical resident of victimhood took a momentary event and turned it into a lifestyle. Consequently, most of their life is now flavored by that event that encouraged them to move into victimhood.

It will show up in their talk, "you make me so angry."

In their thoughts, "I just knew I was going to get hurt again"

In their decisions, "I didn't try because I knew I would fail"

You can never win while living in victimhood. It is impossible to be both victorious and a victim.

"The Spirit of the Sovereign Lord is on me, because the Lord has anointed me to proclaim good news to the poor. He has sent me to bind up the brokenhearted, to proclaim freedom for the captives and release from darkness for the prisoners."

— Isaiah 61:1, NKJV

I am sure when Isaiah mouthed these words, he had no idea the extreme importance they would carry. Hundreds of years later Jesus would walk into the temple and he would stand up to read. A servant would deliver a scroll to him, he would turn to this passage and read it aloud. Jesus reads the versus he felt led to read and then declared that today these words are fulfilled.

The demonic realm was so angered they sought to take Jesus and throw him over the wall of the city. That same demonic realm doesn't want you to move out of victimhood. But know this, Jesus came for captives and prisoners. You can and will be free.

Captives and prisoners are two very different groups of people, but they have some similarities.

Neither can go where they want to go or do what they want to do or be what they want to be. Does that describe the condition you find yourself in?

Being in prison is not a nice experience, and don't doubt it for a moment victimhood is a prison.

Though there are many similarities with captives and prisoners what is different is how they got there.

A prisoner goes to prison because of something they have done.

A captive goes to prison because of something someone else has done.

There are people reading this that have moved into victimhood and are now trapped there because of the words or actions of another.

It is the most devious plot ever devised by our adversary. When you believe you are a victim you are living in victimhood. The actions of another person are the cause of your pain and being a victim, your adversary will convince you that only the actions of that person can heal you. You think if they would just apologize, if they would just treat you right your pain would go away.

Do you see what a bondage that is? In other words, the person who didn't care enough about you to not hurt you, you must now look to them to be your savior. I want to tell you, you don't need them to be free from your pain.

So how do you get free?

You begin by repenting for allowing the voice of your pain to be louder and more real than the voice of God who says I love you and I have nothing but good for your life. If you've been blaming God for this pain, then repent of that also. He did not do this to you. It was not his will that it happened.

Begin to ask the Holy Spirit to give you a word about the situation and then begin to speak that word over yourself. His words are spirit and they are life. They are like a river of living water that flows from him to you and they are empowered as you speak them. You have believed a lie about yourself and the only way to counter that light is to begin to speak the truth. Doing so allows you to become intimate with the truth and the truth always set you free. Guaranteed.

9

DUE SEASON

This chapter is aimed at a very specific person. It is a person that believes God has something better for them but they are losing hope it will ever arrive.

The Bible tells us that when our hope has waited longer than we expected, hope begins to slip away and our heart becomes sick. This heart sickness shows up in a lack of zest for life, depression, and our communication taking on a very negative tone. When our heart gets full of something it comes out of our mouth and if our heart is sick our words become sick. We are irritable, we see no good thing in others and we are quick to criticize. If our heart stays in that condition for long we become judgmental and religious. Joy is nothing but a memory. Worship, if there is any, is robotic and without passion. If this doesn't get fixed, we will lose hope and we desperately need that hope. Faith is a creative force that takes our hope and brings the desire of God to us. But if we lose hope there will be no faith and without faith it is impossible to please God.

We often make the mistake of thinking that because we received a word from God about a matter that it's going to show up any moment now. That is just not how it works. I am going to tell you exactly when God is going to fulfill his promise to you.

"To everything there is a season, A time for every purpose under heaven:"

— ECCLESIASTES 3:1, NKJV

In the original Hebrew language that word everything means everything. That which you were hoping for has a season attached to it. You will not receive it before that due date nor will you receive it late. It will arrive exactly when it supposed to arrive.

"He has made everything beautiful in its time. Also He has put eternity in their hearts, except that no one can find out the work that God does from beginning to end."

— ECCLESIASTES 3:11, NKJV

This promise from God to you is not delayed. It has not arrived because God does nothing average. Everything he does is good and is intended to last for all of eternity. When his promise arrives to you it will be beautiful and you will know the reason for the delay.

"And let us not grow weary while doing good, for in **due season** we shall reap if we do not lose heart."

— GALATIANS 6:9, NKJV

My dear friend you are doing good, please do not grow weary. This miracle headed your way has a due season attached to it and that is exactly when it's going to come. God has not forgotten you he has not forgotten his promise to you. Due season has not yet arrived. But it will. Guaranteed.